FAMOUS ATHLETES

AARON RODGERS

by Tracy Nelson Maurer

Gail Saunders-Smith, PhD, Consulting Editor

Pebble
Plus

CAPSTONE PRESS
a capstone imprint

Pebble Plus is published by Capstone Press,
1710 Roe Crest Drive, North Mankato, Minnesota 56003
www.capstonepub.com

Library of Congress Cataloging-in-Publication Data
Maurer, Tracy, 1965–
 Aaron Rodgers / by Tracy Nelson Maurer.
   pages cm.—(Pebble Plus. Famous Athletes.)
 Includes bibliographical references and index.
 Audience: Age: 5–7.
 Audience: Grade: K to Grade 3.
 ISBN 978-1-4914-6234-8 (library binding)—ISBN 978-1-4914-6250-8 (ebook pdf)—
ISBN 978-1-4914-6254-6 (Pebble Books) paperback)
1. Rodgers, Aaron, 1983– —Juvenile literature. 2. Football players—United States—
Biography—Juvenile literature. 3. Quarterbacks (Football)—United States—Biography—
Juvenile literature. I. Title.
 GV939.R6235M38 2016
 796.332—dc23 [B]   2015001933

Editorial Credits
Erika L. Shores, editor; Juliette Peters, designer; Eric Gohl, media researcher;
Lori Barbeau, production specialist

Photo Credits
AP Photo: David Stluka, 5; Dreamstime: Jerry Coli, cover; Getty Images: Joe Robbins, 15; Newscom: Cal Sport Media/Margaret Bowles, 1, 22, Icon SMI/Icon Sports Media, 17, Icon SMI/Michael Pimente, 13, Icon SMI/Tom Hauck, 11, MCT/Sam Riche, 7, SportsChrome/Bryan Yablonsky, 19, USA Today Sports/Jeff Hanisch, 21; Photo by Chico Enterprise-Record, reprinted with permission: 9 (bottom); Wikimedia: WynterSun12, 9 (top)

Design Elements: Shutterstock

Note to Parents and Teachers

The Famous Athletes set supports national curriculum standards for social studies related to people, places, and culture. This book describes and illustrates Aaron Rodgers. The images support early readers in understanding the text. The repetition of words and phrases helps early readers learn new words. This book also introduces early readers to subject-specific vocabulary words, which are defined in the Glossary section. Early readers may need assistance to read some words and to use the Table of Contents, Glossary, Read More, Internet Sites, Critical Thinking Using the Common Core, and Index sections of the book.

Printed in the United States of America in North Mankato, Minnesota.
042015   008823CGF15

TABLE OF CONTENTS

A Football Family 4
College Teams. 10
Leading the Pack 14

Glossary 22
Read More 23
Internet Sites 23
Critical Thinking
Using the Common Core 24
Index 24

A FOOTBALL FAMILY

Aaron Charles Rodgers was born December 2, 1983. His father, Ed, played football in college. He taught the game to Aaron and his brothers, Luke and Jordan.

1983

born in Chico, California

Aaron Rodgers with his family after winning the 2011 Super Bowl

Aaron has always loved football.

As a kid he watched NFL games

for hours. He drew game plans

in his own playbook.

Aaron dreamed of becoming

an NFL quarterback.

NFL stands for National Football League.

1983

born in Chico,
California

6

Aaron played soccer, basketball,

and baseball as a teenager.

He was also the quarterback

for his high school football team.

Aaron passed for 2,303 yards

in one season to set a record.

1983

2001

born in Chico,
California

sets his school's
football passing
record

PLEASANT VALLEY SENIOR HIGH SCHOOL VIKINGS

AARON 2002

30

9

COLLEGE TEAMS

After high school, Aaron went
to Butte College near
his hometown. As quarterback,
he led the football team
to a winning season.

1983 born in Chico, California

2001 sets his school's football passing record

2002 plays for Butte College

In 2003 Aaron agreed to play

for the University of California,

Berkeley. Aaron would be

the school's quarterback

for the next two years.

1983
born in Chico, California

2001
sets his school's football passing record

2002
plays for Butte College

2003–2004
plays for University of California, Berkeley

13

LEADING THE PACK

Aaron entered the 2005 NFL Draft.

The Green Bay Packers chose

him in the first round.

He would play backup to

star quarterback Brett Favre.

1983 born in Chico, California

2001 sets his school's football passing record

2002 plays for Butte College

2003–2004 plays for University of California, Berkeley

2005 joins Green Bay Packers

In 2008 Brett Favre left

the team. Aaron finally became

a starting NFL quarterback.

His first season was hard.

The Packers won just six games.

But Aaron played well.

1983	2001	2002	2003–2004	2005	2008
born in Chico, California	sets his school's football passing record	plays for Butte College	plays for University of California, Berkeley	joins Green Bay Packers	starts as quarterback for Green Bay Packers

Aaron had an outstanding
third season. He and the Packers
won the Super Bowl. Aaron was
named Super Bowl MVP.

MVP stands for Most Valuable Player.

| 1983 | 2001 | 2002 | 2003–2004 | 2005 | 2008 | 2011 |
| born in Chico, California | sets his school's football passing record | plays for Butte College | plays for University of California, Berkeley | joins Green Bay Packers | starts as quarterback for Green Bay Packers | wins Super Bowl XLV |

19

In 2014 Aaron threw
his 226th touchdown pass
in the NFL. Aaron also led
the Packers to the playoffs.
He earned the season's
MVP award.

1983	2001	2002	2003–2004	2005	2008	2011	2014
born in Chico, California	sets his school's football passing record	plays for Butte College	plays for University of California, Berkeley	joins Green Bay Packers	starts as quarterback for Green Bay Packers	wins Super Bowl XLV	named season's MVP

GLOSSARY

draft—an event held for teams to choose new people to play for them

passing—the act of throwing a ball to another player

playbook—a book of game plans

playoffs—the games that decide which teams go to the championship

quarterback—the player who runs a football team's offense; the quarterback can run, hand off the ball, or make a pass

record—when something is done better than anyone has ever done it before

round—one of the series of repeated sessions to choose players in a draft

season—the time of year in which football games are played

READ MORE

Frisch, Aaron. *Aaron Rodgers.* Mankato, Minn: Creative Education, 2013.

Nagelhout, Ryan. *Aaron Rodgers.* Today's Great Quarterbacks. New York: Gareth Stevens, 2014.

Sandler, Michael. *Aaron Rodgers and the Green Bay Packers: Super Bowl XLV.* New York: Bearport, 2012.

INTERNET SITES

FactHound offers a safe, fun way to find Internet sites related to this book. All of the sites on FactHound have been researched by our staff.

Here's all you do:

Visit *www.facthound.com*

Type in this code: 9781491462348

Super-cool stuff! Check out projects, games and lots more at
www.capstonekids.com

23

CRITICAL THINKING
USING THE COMMON CORE

1. What did Aaron Rodgers do as a child that showed his love of football? (Key Ideas and Details)

2. Why is the quarterback an important member of a football team? (Integration of Knowledge and Ideas)

INDEX

birth, 4
brothers, 4
colleges, 4, 10, 12
draft, 14
father, 4
Favre, Brett, 14, 16
Green Bay Packers, 14, 16, 18, 20

high school, 8, 10
MVP awards, 18, 20
passing, 8, 20
playbooks, 6
quarterback, 6, 8, 10, 12, 14, 16
records, 8
Super Bowl, 18

Word Count: 234
Grade: 1
Early-Intervention Level: 17